Ways Into RE

Belonging

Louise Spilsbury

W
FRANKLIN WATTS
LONDON•SYDNEY

First published in 2010 by
Franklin Watts
338 Euston Road
London NW1 3BH

Franklin Watts Australia
Level 17/207 Kent Street
Sydney NSW 2000

Copyright © Franklin Watts 2010
All rights reserved.

ISBN 978 0 7496 9563 7
Dewey classification number: 200

Series editor: Julia Bird
Art director: Jonathan Hair
Design: Shobha Mucha
Consultant: Joyce Mackley, RE Advisor at RE Today

A CIP catalogue record for this book is available
from the British Library.

Picture credits:
Art Directors & Trip/Alamy: 24; David Ball/Alamy: 10t;
Andi Berger/Shutterstock: 18t; Christophe Boisvieux/Corbis: 14;
Brand X Pictures/Getty Images: 13; Robert Dodge/istockphoto: 25;
Chris Fairclough: 18-19b; Jeff Greenberg/Alamy: 15;
Julien Grondin/istockphoto: 11t; Robert Harding PL/Corbis: 19;
Bonnie Jacobs/istockphoto: 6b; Martin Kucera/Shutterstock: 9b;
Juan Mabromata/Getty Images: 18b; Fred Mayer/Getty Images: 17;
Franky de Meyer/istockphoto: 7b; John Moore/Getty Images: 12t;
Mikhail Nekrasov/istockphoto: 10b; Christine Osborne/Corbis: 11b;
Christine Osborne/World Religions PL: 23t; Edward Parker/Alamy: 7t;
Radius Images/Alamy: 27; Gary Roebuck/Alamy: 22t; RonTech2000/istockphoto: 23b;
D R A Schwarz/istockphoto: 6t; Paula Solloway/ALamy: 20b;
Wendy Stone/Corbis: 16; sunny 13/istockphoto: 20t;
World Religions PL/Alamy: cover, 8, 9t; Alison Wright/Corbis: 21.
Lisa Kyle Young/istockphoto: 12b.

Every attempt has been made to clear copyright.
Should there be any inadvertent omission,
please apply to the publisher for rectification.

Printed in China

Franklin Watts is a division of Hachette Children's Books,
an Hachette UK company.
www.hachette.co.uk

Contents

What does it mean to belong?	6
When you first belong	8
Sharing beliefs	10
Important people	12
A way of life	14
Special days	16
Worshipping together	18
Showing you belong	20
Sharing food	22
Funeral services	24
Think about belonging	26
The six main faiths	28
Useful words	29
Index	30
About this book	30

What does it mean to belong?

To belong means to be a member of a group or community.

Most of us belong to a family. Who are the people who belong to your family?

Some people belong to a sports team too. What teams or groups do you belong to?

What feels special about belonging?

Some people belong to a religious group.

The religion of Islam teaches that all Muslims are members of one big family.

Christians think of themselves as a family, with God as their father.

Why do you think religions think of themselves as a family?

7

When you first belong

Some people belong to a religious family from the day they are born, because of their parents. Most religions have ceremonies to welcome a new baby.

A Muslim father whispers to his baby about how special God is for Muslims. When Muslim babies are seven days old, they are given special Muslim names.

Do you know what your name means?

To name a Sikh baby, the Sikh holy book is opened on any page. The parents choose a name that begins with the first letter of a verse on that page.

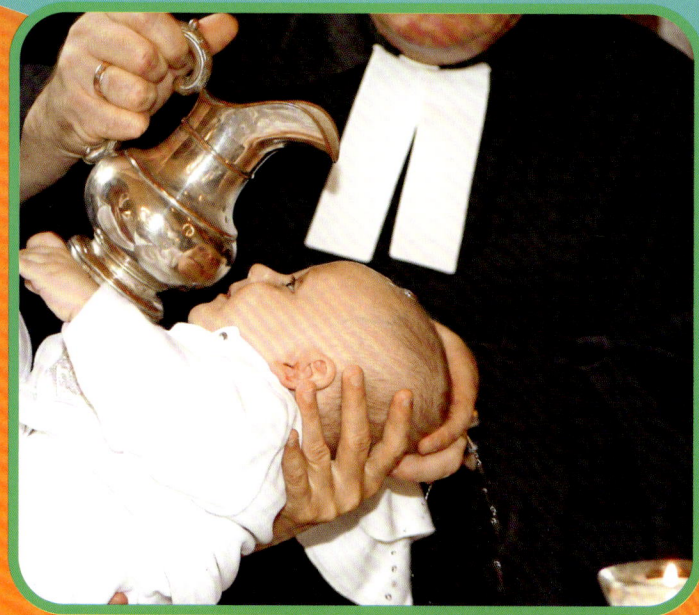

Christians welcome a baby into the Christian faith by baptising him or her. In a baptism ceremony, water is poured over the baby's head.

Talk about...
...why ceremonies like baptisms are important. How do they help to make us feel that we belong?

Sharing beliefs

People from the same religion share many of the same beliefs. This helps them to feel like they belong to a big family.

Christians believe in God. They follow the teachings of God's son Jesus Christ.

Hindus believe in one God who takes many forms. This is Ganesha, the elephant-headed god.

Buddhists follow the teachings of a man they call the Buddha who lived about 2,500 years ago.

Sikhs believe in one God and follow the teachings of Gurus. Gurus were people whom Sikhs believe passed on God's teachings.

Who helps religious people to learn about and understand their faith? Turn the page to find out.

Important people

Religious leaders are important people. They help people to belong to a faith.

Muslim leaders are called imams. Imams lead prayers in the mosque and hold services such as weddings and funerals.

Christian leaders are called vicars, ministers or priests. They lead worship in churches. They also lead marriages and funerals.

How do you think it would feel to be a leader? Why are leaders important?

People who help Hindus worship are called priests. Hindu priests lead worship. They also look after the temple and the shrine where people worship.

Talk about...

...other leaders in your community and what they do to help people. You could include: •teachers •sports coaches •doctors •Brownie or Cub leaders

A way of life

When people belong to a religion it affects the way they act and behave. Holy books teach people how they should live and give them rules to live by.

The Muslim holy book is the Qu'ran. It is written in Arabic. Muslims believe it contains messages from the Muslim God, Allah.

Talk about...
...what rules you follow at home. Who makes the rules? Why do you think we have rules?

Religions teach people
to help each other and others.

Christians often collect money during
the church service. The money is used to keep
the church in good repair and to help people
who are in need.

How do you choose the right way to behave and to live?

Special days

People from some religions share a special day every week. On this day, they gather with their family and spend some time thinking about God.

Friday is an important day for Muslims. On Fridays, male Muslims often gather at the mosque for prayers.

Jews believe that God made the world in six days and rested on the seventh day. So on Saturdays, or Shabbat, many Jews do not work. They worship and share a special meal together.

Why is it important to have times of rest? How do you spend your days of rest?

Why do people worship together? Turn the page to find out.

Worshipping together

Worshipping together gives people a sense of belonging.

Christians pray together as a way of talking to God.

The Mool Mantar is a special Sikh prayer that describes God. Sikhs say it together.

What things do you do that make you feel you belong?

Most religious people meet together in special places to worship.

Hindus meet and worship together in a temple called a mandir.

Do you have a special place? Why do you go there? How might a special place to worship make people feel they belong?

What else do people do to show they belong? Turn the page to find out.

Showing you belong

Religious people may wear special clothes to show that they belong.

Many Sikhs wear a turban. It reminds them and other people about their belief in God.

Some Muslim girls and women wear a headscarf called a hijab as a sign of their faith.

Buddhist monks wear orange, red, pink or yellow robes. They use prayer beads to count the mantras they say. Mantras are special words that help Buddhists think about Buddha's teachings.

Talk about...
...what you wear or carry to show that you belong.
Include things like:
- school uniform
- badges
- dance kit
- sports kit
- football shirt
- team shirts

How do you feel when you wear your special clothes or uniforms?

Sharing food

People of some different religions eat certain foods to show they belong.

Many Muslims do not eat anything that is from a pig, such as bacon. They only eat meat that has been prepared in a special way. This is called halal.

Many Hindus are vegetarians. They do not eat meat or fish. Most Hindus do not eat beef because they believe cows are holy and should not be harmed.

Look at these two pictures.

What is the same and what is different? What do you think the people are talking about?

Langar is the meal that Sikhs share after worship.

A picnic with friends.

How does sharing meals with people make us feel we belong?

Funeral services

When someone dies, most religions hold a special goodbye service called a funeral.

When a Muslim dies, the whole community comes to the funeral, because they believe that all Muslims belong together.

How do we remember loved ones who have died?

Gravestones mark where people are buried in a cemetery. Some people leave flowers to show that they remember the people who are buried there.

Talk about…
…why it is important to talk about and remember people who belonged to us.

Think about belonging

Think about how belonging makes us feel special. Make a spider diagram like this. Then fill in the spaces. Write all the people, groups or communities you belong to in one circle. Then write how belonging to them makes you feel special in the circle next to it. This one has been done to show you how.

- My family make me feel special because they know me the best.
- **Family**
- School makes me feel special because I learn and have fun with my friends there.
- **School**
- **How belonging makes me feel**
- **Friends**
- **Basketball team**
- Friends make me feel special because they understand how I feel.
- My basketball team makes me feel special because I like being part of a team.

Find out what difference belonging to a religion makes to people's lives. Write down some questions you could ask. Try to ask people from different religions the same questions. What do you find out?

After you have done this, write one or two sentences about what is special about belonging.

The six main faiths

The world's six main faiths are Hinduism, Islam, Christianity, Sikhism, Buddhism and Judaism. Each of the six main faiths have different beliefs:

Hindus believe there is one God who can take different forms. Hindus worship these different gods and goddesses.

Christians believe there is one God who has three parts: The Father, the Son and the Holy Spirit. Jesus is the son of God and was sent to Earth to save people.

Buddhists do not worship a God. They follow the teachings of a man called Buddha and try to live in the way he taught.

Muslims follow the religion of Islam. They follow five rules known as the Five Pillars: to believe in one God – Allah, to pray five times a day, to fast during the month of Ramadan, to give money to the poor and to go on pilgrimage to Makkah.

Jews believe that there is one God who made everything and that they should follow Jewish law.

Sikhs believe that there is one God who made everything. They follow the teachings of ten Gurus (teachers) who told people what God wanted.

Useful words

Baptism – a service to welcome someone into the Christian church. Babies, children and adults can be baptised.

Ceremony – a gathering to celebrate or mark an important event or time. Weddings and funerals are types of ceremony.

Community – a group of people who live together in a certain area or who are part of the same religion, school or team. Muslims feel they are part of a world Muslim community.

Halal – usually describes meat that has been prepared in a special way. Halal means something that is permitted by Islamic law.

Holy book – an important book that has teachings or stories about a religion. The Bible is the Christian holy book.

Mandir – a building where Hindus meet for worship.

Mosque – a building where Muslims meet for worship.

Prayer – special words people say to speak to, give thanks to or ask for help from God. The Lord's prayer is an important Christian prayer.

Religion – belief in a God or gods. Islam and Christianity are two religions.

Service – when a religious leader leads people in worship or in a special ceremony.

Shrine – building or place that is holy. Many shrines have objects that represent one god or goddess.

Turban – headdress made by winding a long piece of cloth many times around the head.

Worship – to show respect or love for God or gods. Some people worship by praying and singing.

Index

baptism 9
beliefs 10–11, 20
clothes 20–21
days of rest 17
food 22–23
funerals 24–25

holy books 14
naming ceremonies 8–9
religious leaders 12–13
special places 19
worshipping 12, 13, 17, 18–19

About this book

- Ways into RE is designed to develop children's knowledge of the world's main faiths and to help them respect different religions, beliefs, values and traditions and understand how they influence society and the world. This title Belonging is a way in for children to draw on their understanding of belonging, and relate it to different faiths.

- It will help if the children have had previous opportunities to discuss and think about the idea of belonging. On pages 6–7 they could talk about what belonging means to them and use a word bank to say what groups they belong to or they could complete a family tree. Explain the wider meaning of 'family' in a religious context.

- It might help children's understanding of initiation ceremonies (pages 8–9) if they could talk about the way non-religious groups welcome new members too, such as Brownie or Cub ceremonies.

- To help children with their general understanding of world religions (introduced in pages 10–11 and 14–15), they could read and refer to page 28, which has a brief description of the six main faiths. Together they could discuss the similarities and differences between the religions.

- When talking about what people do to show they belong (pages 18–23) you could ask class members who belong to a faith to describe what they and their families do and wear to show that they belong to a faith group. Children could also draw clothing or symbols from a faith that interests them and write a description of what it is and means.

- If children cannot interview people from different faiths (26–27) they could watch DVD interviews and discussions to help them come to an understanding of what is special about belonging to a religion for a believer. They could list the ways belonging to a religion affects all aspects of a person's life, from what they wear and eat, to their weekly schedule and where they go.